LISZT

SIX CONSOLATIONS

S. 172
FOR THE PIANO

AN ALFRED MASTERWORK EDITION

Alfred Music Publishing Co., Inc.
P.O. Box 10003
Van Nuys, CA 91410-0003
alfred.com

Book Alone:
ISBN-10: 0-7390-3309-3
ISBN-13: 978-0-7390-3309-8
Book & CD:
ISBN-10: 0-7390-7759-7
ISBN-13: 978-0-7390-7759-7

Cover art: Golden Autumn, 1895
by Isaac Levitan (1860–1900)
Tretyakov Gallery, Moscow, Russia
Scala/Art Resource, New York

FRANZ LISZT
Six Consolations, S. 172

Edited by Maurice Hinson

CONTENTS

This edition is dedicated to
Mr. and Mrs. Nathaniel
Patch, with admiration
and appreciation.

Maurice Hinson

Foreword

Franz Liszt (1811–1886) composed these diminutive pieces in 1849, although their earliest form may date from the first half of the 1840s. This is indicated by the date January 5, 1844 on the autograph manuscript of the fifth piece, *Madrigal*. This early form of the fifth piece is quite different from the final version[1] used in this collection. The 1849 version of *Six Consolations*, S. 172 was first published in 1850 in Leipzig by Breitkopf and Härtel and has become the best-known of Liszt's smaller piano works. This group of pieces was presumably inspired by the title of Sainte-Beuve's collection of poems *Les Consolations*, dating from 1830. These poems expressed themes of unfulfilled hope. Charles Sainte-Beuve was the pseudonym of the French literary historian Joseph Delorme (1804–1869). The melody of no. 4 is ascribed to Grand Duchess Maria Pavlovna, sister of Tsar Nicholas I and mother of Liszt's Weimar patron, Grand Duke Carl Alexander.

Liszt may have intended all six of these lyrical miniatures to be performed as a group, but various groupings are effective such as nos. 1, 2; 1, 2, 4, 6; or 4, 5, 6. Single numbers may also be performed or combined with groupings of other works.

The following table shows Liszt's organization of the six-piece group plus approximate performance times for each piece:

The mood or character of "consoling" permeates the entire set and reminds this editor of Mendelssohn's *Songs without Words*, Op. 30, No. 3, "Consolation," which was first published in 1835. Liszt's pieces are related to some of Mendelssohn's pieces as well as to some of Chopin's nocturnes. No. 3 especially seems to have been inspired by Chopin's *Nocturne*, Op. 27, No. 2. Even though a lyrical quality is found throughout the *Six Consolations*, each piece is distinctive. This set provides an excellent introduction to Liszt's melodic style, pianistic treatment and harmonic idiom.

About This Edition

The source for this edition is the Breitkopf and Härtel edition of 1850. Also consulted were the Peters edition edited by Emil Sauer and the New Liszt Edition published by Editio Musica Budapest. All fingerings are editorial. Liszt left pedal indications only for no. 3. These have been retained (𝄑 ❋) and the editor's suggested pedal marks are indicated beneath Liszt's markings. All other pedal indications and parenthetical material are editorial.

Key	Tempo	Meter	Length	Approximate Performance Time
E Major	Andante con moto	𝄴	25 measures	1:10
E Major	Un poco più mosso	𝄴	81 measures	3:00
D-flat Major	Lento placido	𝄴 (against 12/8)	61 measures	4:00
D-flat Major	Quasi adagio	𝄴	34 measures	3:10
E Major	Andantino	3/4	59 measures	2:15
E Major	Allegretto sempre cantabile[2]	3/8 (to 𝄴)	100 measures	3:10

---

1. Preface to *Liszt Piano Works*: Series I, vol. 9, *Various Cyclical Works I*. Budapest: Editio Musica Budapest, 1981, pp. xiii and xiv.

2. John Diercks. "The *Consolations*: delightful things hidden away." *Journal of the American Liszt Society*, vol. III (June 1978):19.

Franz Liszt
(1811–1886)

Archiv für Kunst und Geschichte, London

About the Music

Andante con moto. Form: **A** = measures 1–8; **B** (derived from measure 4) = 8–16; **A**^{1} = 16–25.

This chordal legato piece serves as an introductory meditation and establishes the key of E major as the dominating key of the entire group. It is mainly monothematic and reiterates three contemplative motives: (1) a halting chord sequence (measures 1–4); (2) a similar chord sequence (measures 5–8); and (3) contrasting sigh-figure (measures 9–16). These motives are varied and recur throughout.

Un poco più mosso. Form: **A** = measures 1–29; bridge = 29–37; **A**^{1} = 38–75; coda = 75–81.

This lovely "song without words" soars and contains some unexpected and beautiful modulations (measures 14–16, 19–20, 51–53). Liszt uses one of his favorite devices in dividing the melody between the hands (measures 38–42, 46–52).

Lento placido. Form: **A** = measures 1–18; **A**^{1} = 19–35; **A**^{2} = 35–43; coda = 44–61.

This nocturne, probably the most frequently performed of the group, seems to be inspired by Chopin's *Nocturne*, Op. 27, No. 2, also in D-flat major. Liszt features a right-hand cantilena over left-hand, broken-chord, accompanying figuration. A quiet, pensive and nostalgic mood permeates the piece. The low D-flat in measures 1–9 should be played very quietly in each measure (even though tied) since the pedal changes make it lose its continuous sound.

Another solution to these measures (1–9) is to catch the low D-flat in measure 1 with the sostenuto pedal (middle pedal) and release the sostenuto pedal on beat 3 of measure 9. The damper pedal would also be used as indicated throughout these measures.

Quasi adagio. Form: All material derives from measures 1–4. **A** = measures 1–9; **B** = 10–16; **A**^{1} = 16–25; **A**^{2} (coda) = 25–34.

This piece and no. 1 are the most chordal of the set and are almost prayerlike in mood. The directions *cantabile con devozione* (in a singing style and with devotion) support this character. Play the syncopation in measures 3, 4, 8 and 9 with a bit of rubato. The slow and sustained melody must be well projected throughout, even when in the bass at measures 16–20. In measures 25–27 the left hand should project the melody while the right hand plays the series of four half notes. Roll the chord slowly in measure 32. This beautiful piece is an excellent study in playing chords quietly.

Andantino. Form: Introduction = measures 1–3; **A** = 3–11; **B** = 11–21; **A**^{1} = 21–31; **B**^{1} = 31–46; coda = 46–59.

Continuous cantilena vocal style plus use of parallel thirds and sixths suggest a Mendelssohn "song without words" with flowing accompaniment. Keep the tempo fairly straightforward and avoid excessive use of rubato. Project the left-hand thematic germ from section **A** in measures 44–45 and 47–50.

Allegretto sempre cantabile. Form: **A** = measures 1–18; **A**^{1} = 18–34; **B** = 34–68; **A**^{2} = 69–84; coda = 84–100.

This piece, the longest of the group, is an excellent study for pedaling and arm weight. The melody contains numerous arpeggiated accompanimental chords and moves over an extended range of the keyboard. Take time to play measures 19–68 with great expression. Play measures 93–98 (plus the eighth-note pickup to measure 93) more quietly than measures 85–93. This coda (measures 84–100) recalls the gentle and consoling quality of most of the set and can be played a little slower than the opening section (measures 1–18).

Six Consolations

No. 1

Franz Liszt (1811–1886)
S. 172:1

No. 2

8

9

No. 3

S. 172:3

(a) Liszt's pedal indications.
(b) Editor's pedal indications.

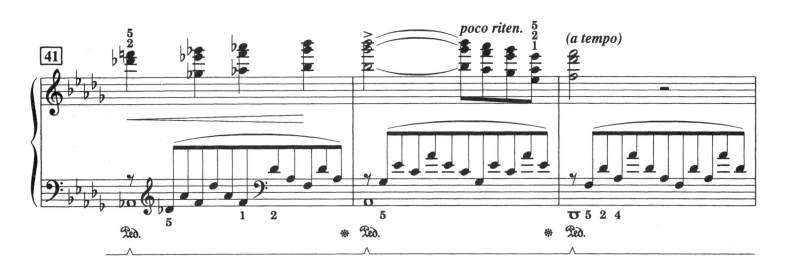

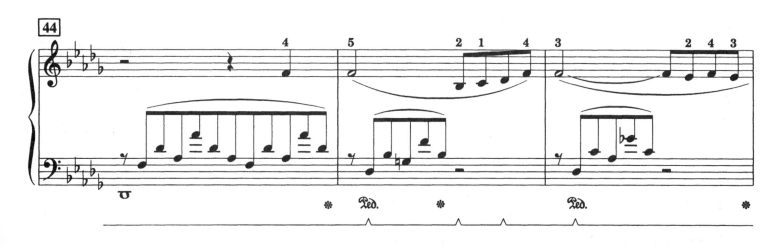

Ⓒ The cadenza figuration may be repeated until the sound is almost gone.

No. 4

S. 172:4

16

No. 5

S. 172:5

(a) Play the grace note before the beat.   (b) Begin the arpeggiated chord on the beat.

No. 6

S. 172:6

LISZT

SIX CONSOLATIONS, S. 172

Philip Thomson, pianist

THE ALFRED MASTERWORK LIBRARY
CD EDITIONS

About the CD Recording

Because music is an art form and not a science, many great pianists, conductors, and even composers vary their interpretations and performances as they gain insight into a work. For this reason, the CD recording within this book may not adhere specifically to the tempo, dynamic, and phrasing indications included in the score. Listening to a fine interpretation of a work is beneficial; however, a well-rounded performance combines musicality as well as stylistically correct performance practices.

Alfred CD Editions with Naxos Recordings:

J. S. Bach: Italian Concerto, BWV 971 (37136)
Bartók: Romanian Folk Dances, Sz. 56 (37158)
Chopin: 14 of His Easiest Piano Selections (28050)
Chopin: 19 of His Most Popular Piano Selections (28048)
Chopin: Preludes (28052)
Chopin: Waltzes (Complete) (28054)
Debussy: Préludes, Book I (37138)
Debussy: Préludes, Book II (37140)
Gershwin: Three Preludes (37146)
Liszt: Six Consolations, S. 172 (37144)
Satie: 3 Gymnopédies & 3 Gnossiennes (28056)
Schubert: Impromptus, Op. 90 (37148)
Schubert: Impromptus, Op. 142 (37150)
Schumann: Carnaval, Op. 9 (37152)
Schumann: Fantasiestücke, Op. 12 (37156)
Schumann: Symphonic Etudes, Op. 13 (37154)
Tcherepnin: Bagatelles, Op. 5 (37134)
Villa-Lobos: A prole do bebê no. 1 (37142)

Alfred Classic Editions with Naxos Recordings:

The Piano Works of Rachmaninoff:
   Volume 1: Preludes (26996)
   Volume 2: Etudes-tableaux (26997)
   Volume 3: Morceaux de salon and Moments musicaux (26998)
   Volume 4: Miscellaneous Pieces (26999)
   Volume 5: Sonatas (27000)
   Volume 6: Variations (27001)
   Volume 7: Transcriptions (27002)
   Volume 9: Piano Duos (27004)
   Volume 10: Symphonic Dances (27005)
   Volume 12: Piano Concerto No. 2 (27007)
   Volume 13: Piano Concerto No. 3 (27008)
   Volume 14: Piano Concerto No. 4 (27009)
   Volume 15: Rhapsody on a Theme of Paganini (27010)

Additional Alfred CD Editions:

J. S. Bach: Anna Magdalena's Notebook (22523)
J. S. Bach: The First Book for Pianists (20854)
J. S. Bach: An Introduction to His Keyboard Music (24456)
J. S. Bach: 18 Short Preludes for the Keyboard (22522)
J. S. Bach: Two-Part Inventions (22528)
J. S. Bach: Inventions and Sinfonias (22521)
Beethoven: The First Book for Pianists (20850)
Burgmüller: 25 Progressive Pieces, Op. 100 (22524)
Chopin: The First Book for Pianists (20848)
Chopin: An Introduction to His Piano Works (22520)
Clementi: Six Sonatinas, Op. 36 (22525)
Debussy: 12 Selected Piano Works (35314)
Debussy: Children's Corner (28058)
Debussy: An Introduction to His Piano Music (24460)
Liszt: 21 Selected Piano Works (26191)
Mozart: The First Book for Pianists (20852)
Mozart: An Introduction to His Keyboard Works (24458)
Rachmaninoff: 10 Selected Piano Works (26193)
Schumann: Album for the Young, Op. 68 (22527)
Schumann: Scenes from Childhood, Op. 15 (22526)
Sonatina Album (22529)

BN 6390B

37144 Book & CD   US $8.99

0 38081 41257 3

alfred.com

ISBN-10: 0-7390-7759-7
ISBN-13: 978-0-7390-7759-7

50899

9 780739 077597

Arcangelo

CORELLI

LA FOLIA

FOR VIOLIN AND PIANO

K 04409